Phonics

Let's make it simple...

Foundational Phonics

Set I
Book 5

Namrata Dhawle

Made with ❤ on the Notion Press Platform
www.notionpress.com

Preface

Since the early 20th century, phonics has been widely used in primary education to teach literacy across the English-speaking world.

This syllabus is designed according to the Montessori methodology, which emphasizes guiding children through techniques that develop their awareness of sounds. Using phonics, we can effectively teach English reading and writing.

Phonics is a method for teaching reading and writing in English by fostering phonemic awareness—the ability to hear, identify, and manipulate phonemes. It establishes a connection between these sounds and the spelling patterns that represent them.

The primary goal of phonics is to enable beginning readers to decode unfamiliar written words by sounding them out or blending the sounds of spelling patterns. Since phonics focuses on spoken and written units within words, it is considered a sub-lexical approach. It is often contrasted with the whole-language philosophy, which adopts a word-level-up strategy for teaching reading.

In essence, phonics teaches reading and pronunciation through the recognition of letter sounds, letter combinations, and syllables.

To implement this learning method, teachers must begin preparing children in the nursery by raising their awareness of sounds. This involves enriching their vocabulary through exposure to small objects or pictures representing various words.

Most importantly, before starting sound games or phonics activities, it is essential to ensure that children are familiar with the words and objects being introduced.

Sincerely,
Namrata Ninad Dhawle
AMI Certified Montessori Educator
Contact:namrata.montessori@gmail.com

Guidelines for Teachers

Daily Teaching Plan :
Teachers are encouraged to be prepared with the teaching plan for the next day according to the syllabus. This will help maintain a smooth and engaging learning experience.

Workbooks Management :
Please ensure that all workbooks are kept in the classrooms to maintain organization and easy accessibility for effective learning.

Classroom Supplies :
Each classroom should be equipped with a set of **slates and chalk or blank papers and crayons** to foster creativity and interactive learning.

Group Activities :
Group activities should involve a maximum of 4-5 children per group to promote effective participation and collaboration while ensuring individual attention.

Additional Support :
Additional revision sessions should be arranged for students who may benefit from extra practice, helping them strengthen their understanding and build confidence.

Puzzle Words Preparation :
Teachers are requested to laminate and cut the provided **Puzzle Words** separately, ensuring that each classroom has one complete set of **Puzzle Words** (Set II Book 1 - Phonogram) to support literacy development.

Thank you for your dedication and commitment to creating a positive and productive learning environment.

Namrata Dhawle

Read and Match

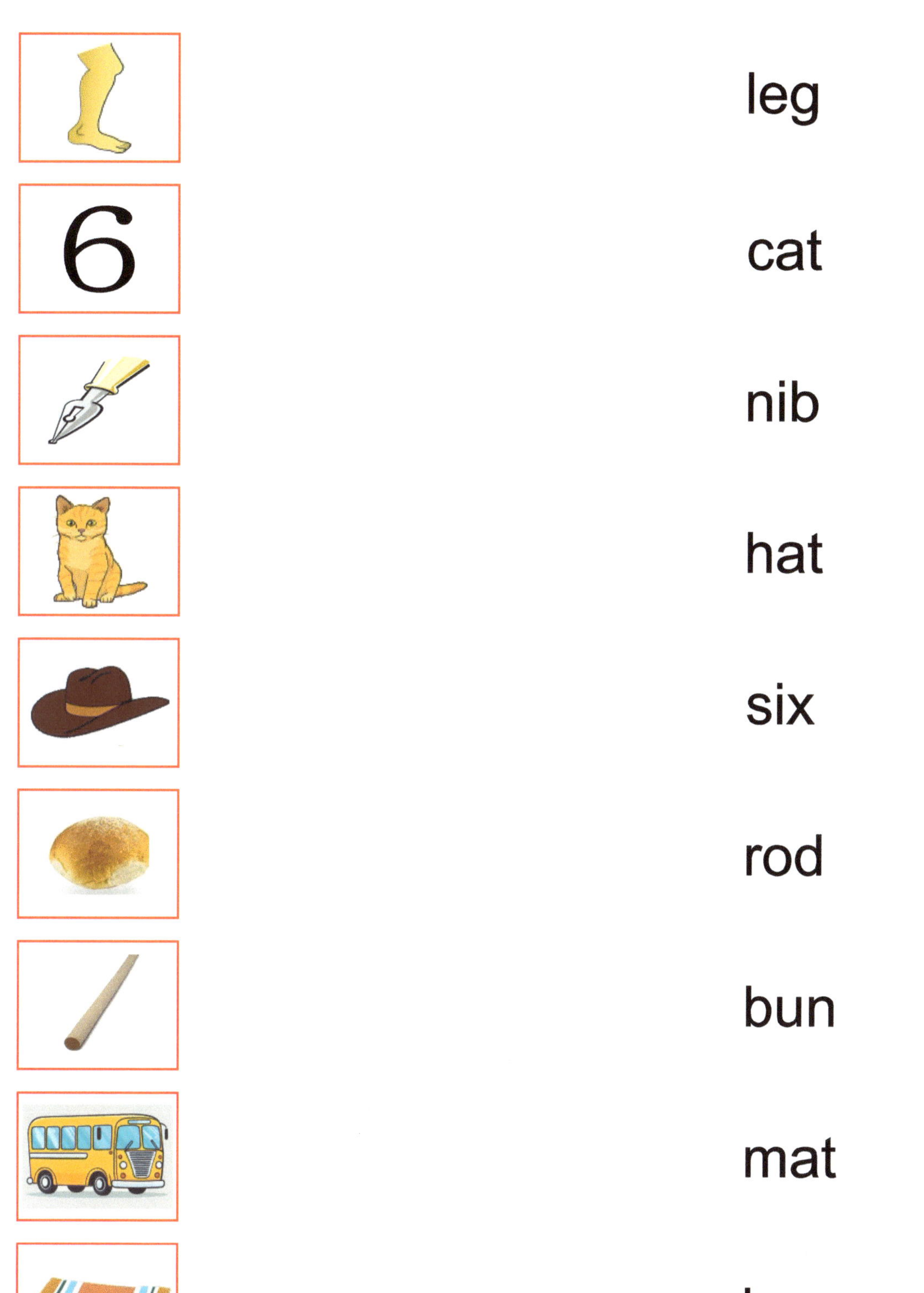

leg

cat

nib

hat

six

rod

bun

mat

bus

Read and Match

Read and Match

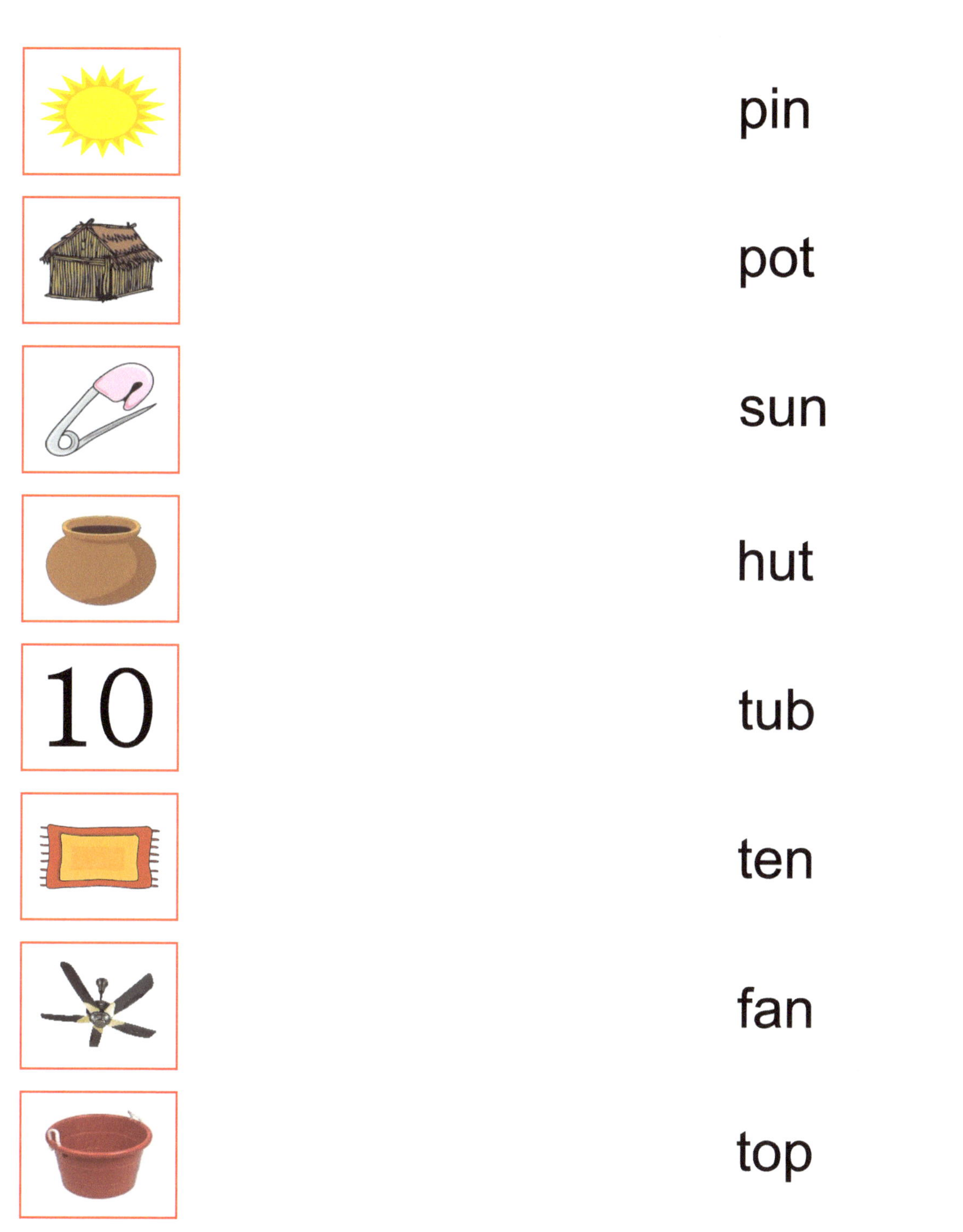

Read and Match

Read and Match

bin

bus

lid

jar

nib

hop

hen

cap

lip

Read and Match

hot

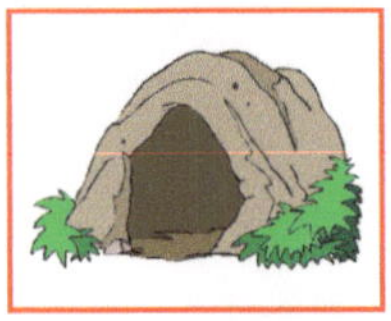

mop

jam

dog

den

pen

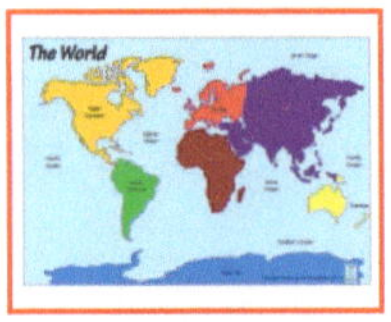

yak

map

cub

Read and Match

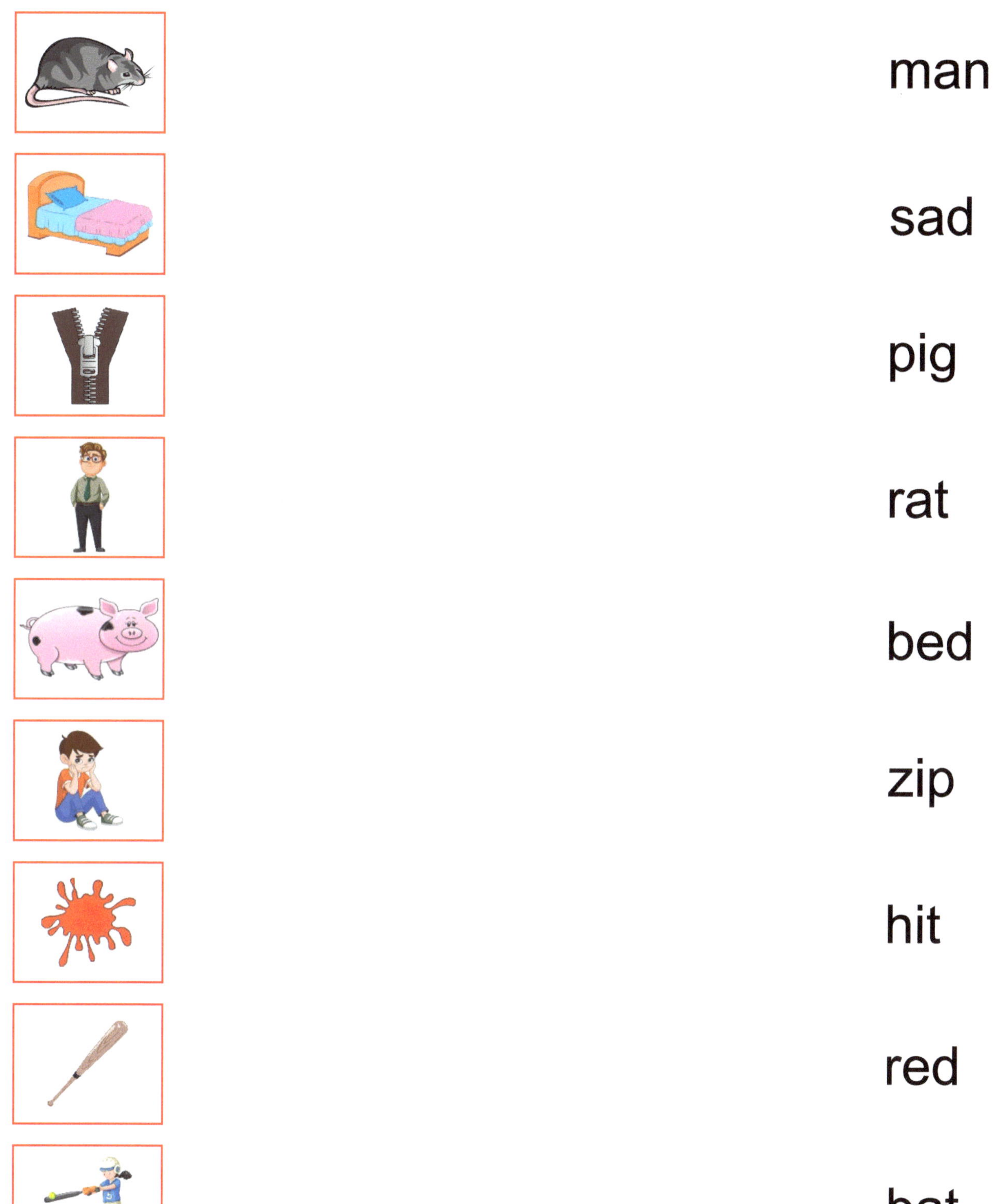

Read and Match

bib

fin

wax

sit

web

wig

can

cup

tap

Read and Match

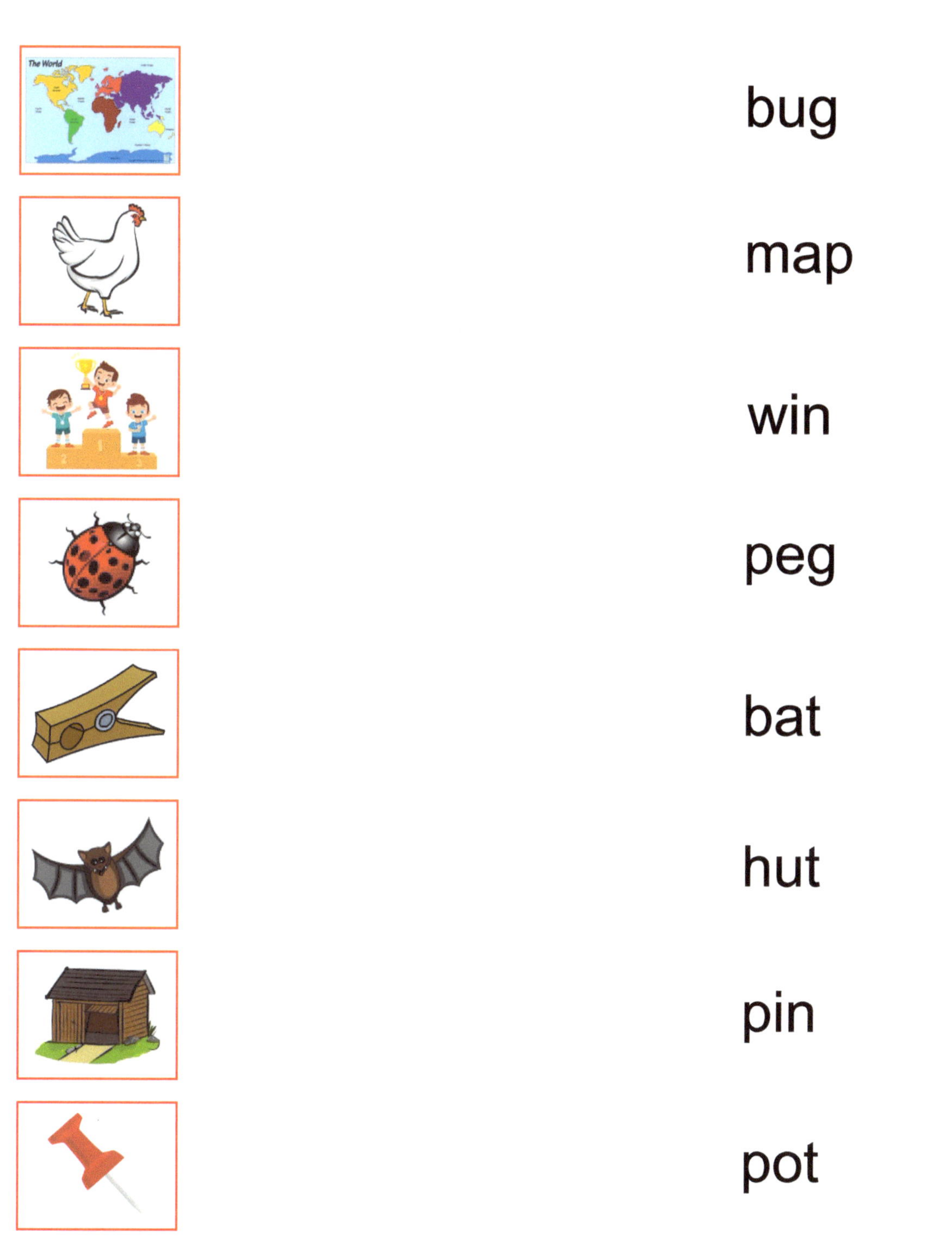

	bug
	map
	win
	peg
	bat
	hut
	pin
	pot
	hen

Read and Match

Read and Match

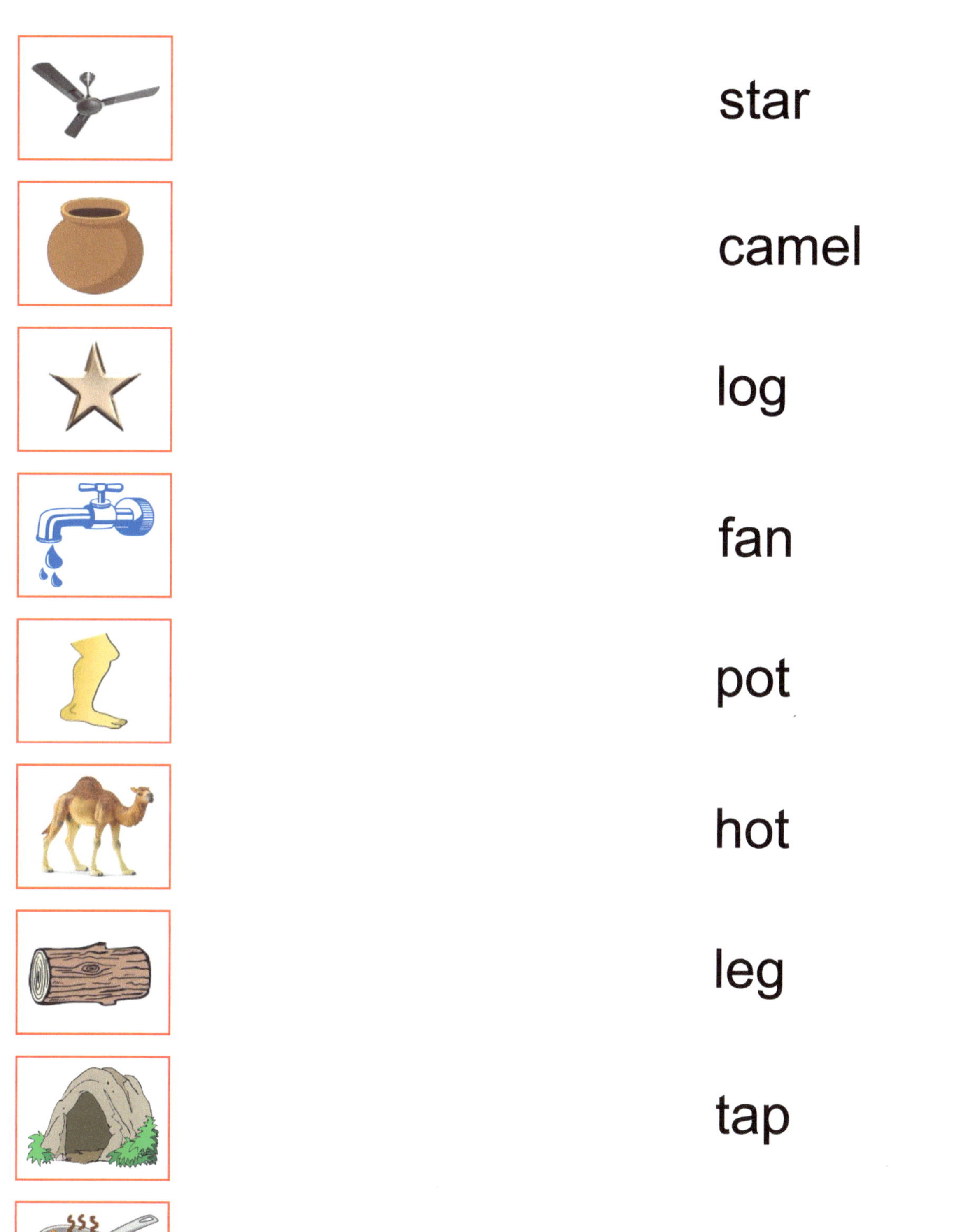

Read and Match

bun

cat

cap

jar

tag

jug

jar

mom

vet

Read and Match

bat

red

hop

hen

cub

yak

map

hit

jam

Read and Match

drum

tent

comb

pant

hand

lips

plum

jet

plus

Read and Match

Read and Match

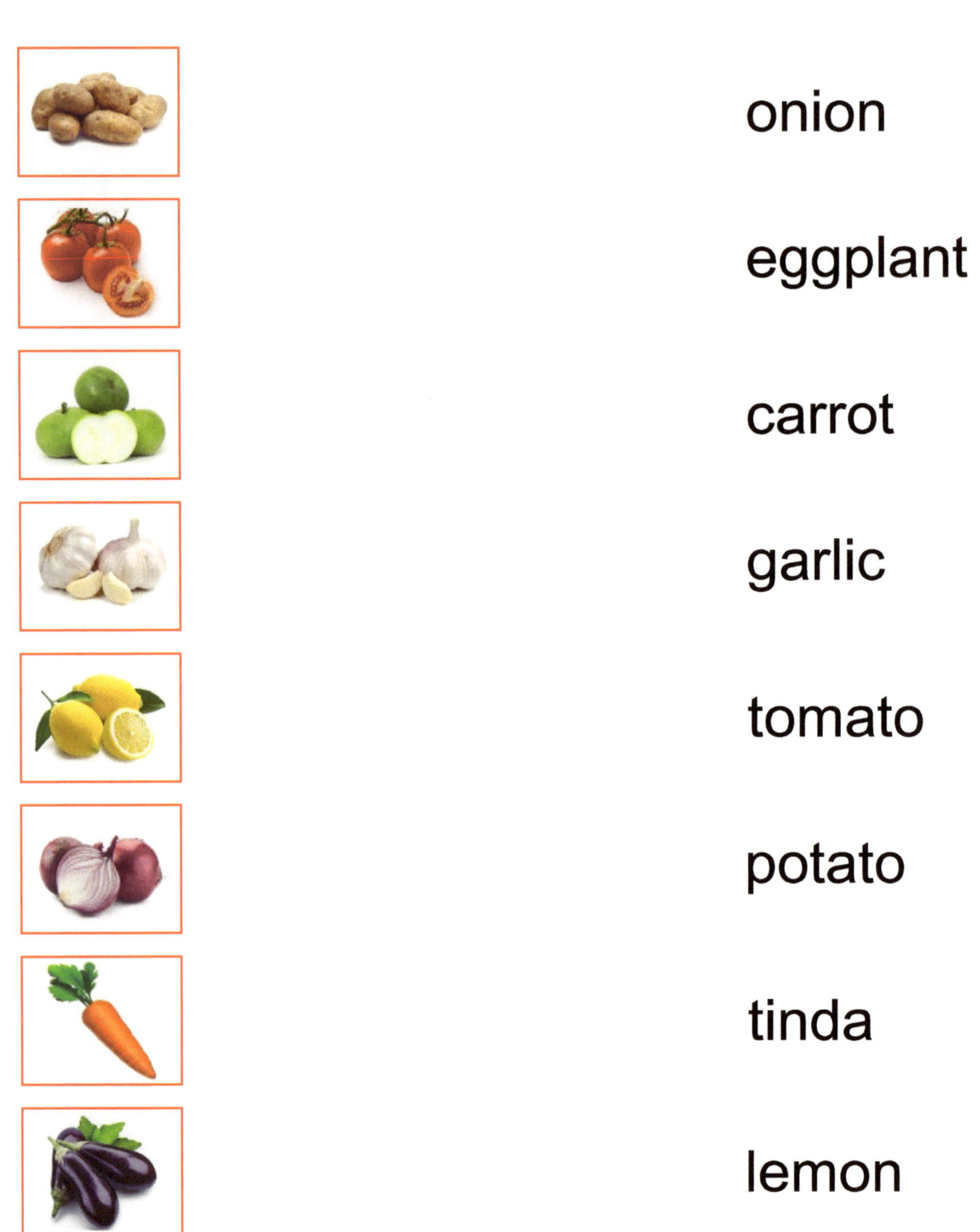

Read and Match

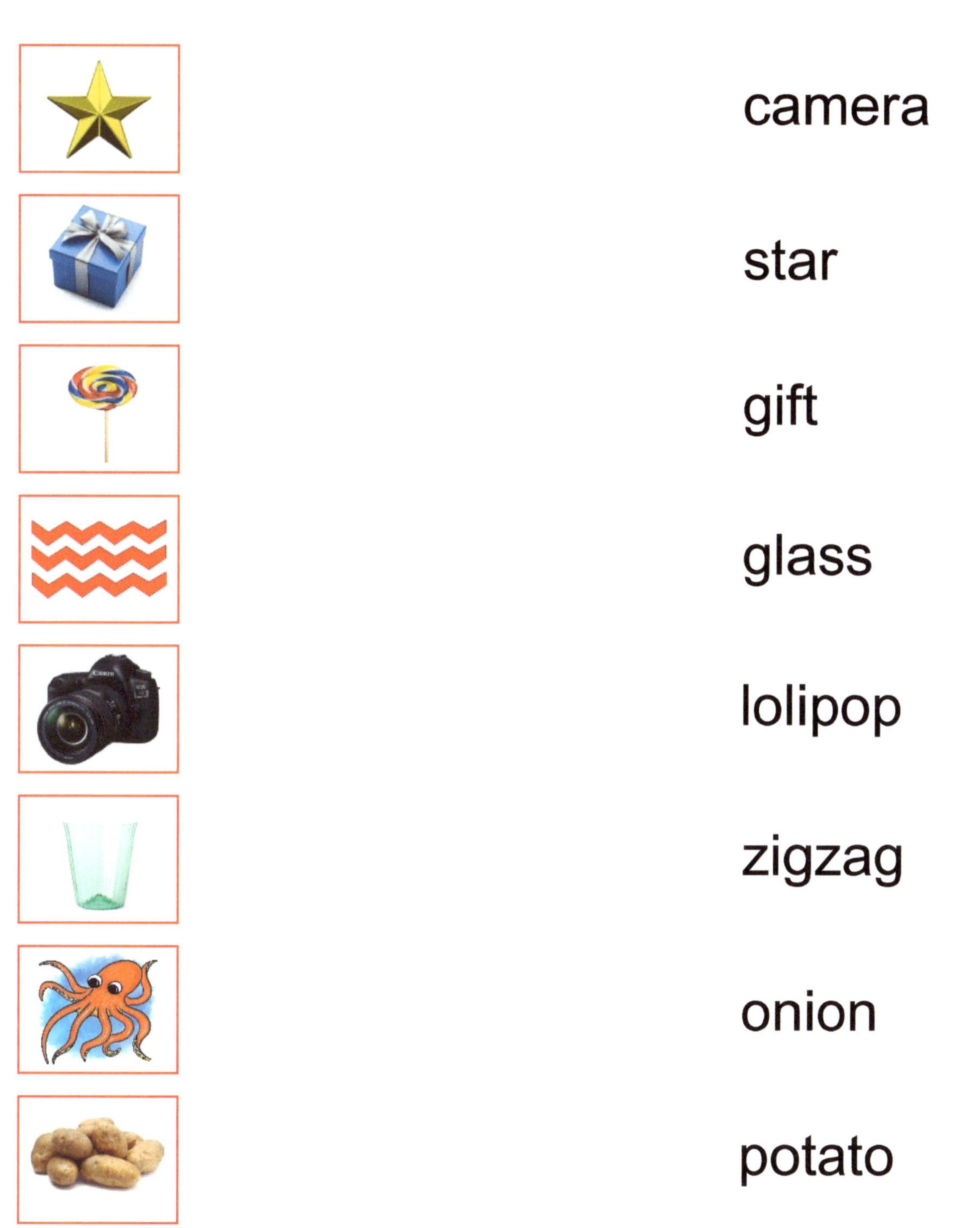

Read and Match

onion

carrot

eggplant

capsicum

potato

tinda

tomato

corn

yam

Read and Match

garlic

potato

pumpkin

beetroot

tomato

lemon

broccoli

mint

dill

Read and Match

octopus

egg

apple

umbrella

igloo

up

ax

lab

ox

Read and Match

seven

corn

sand

lips

tent

top

comb

flag

hand

Read and Match

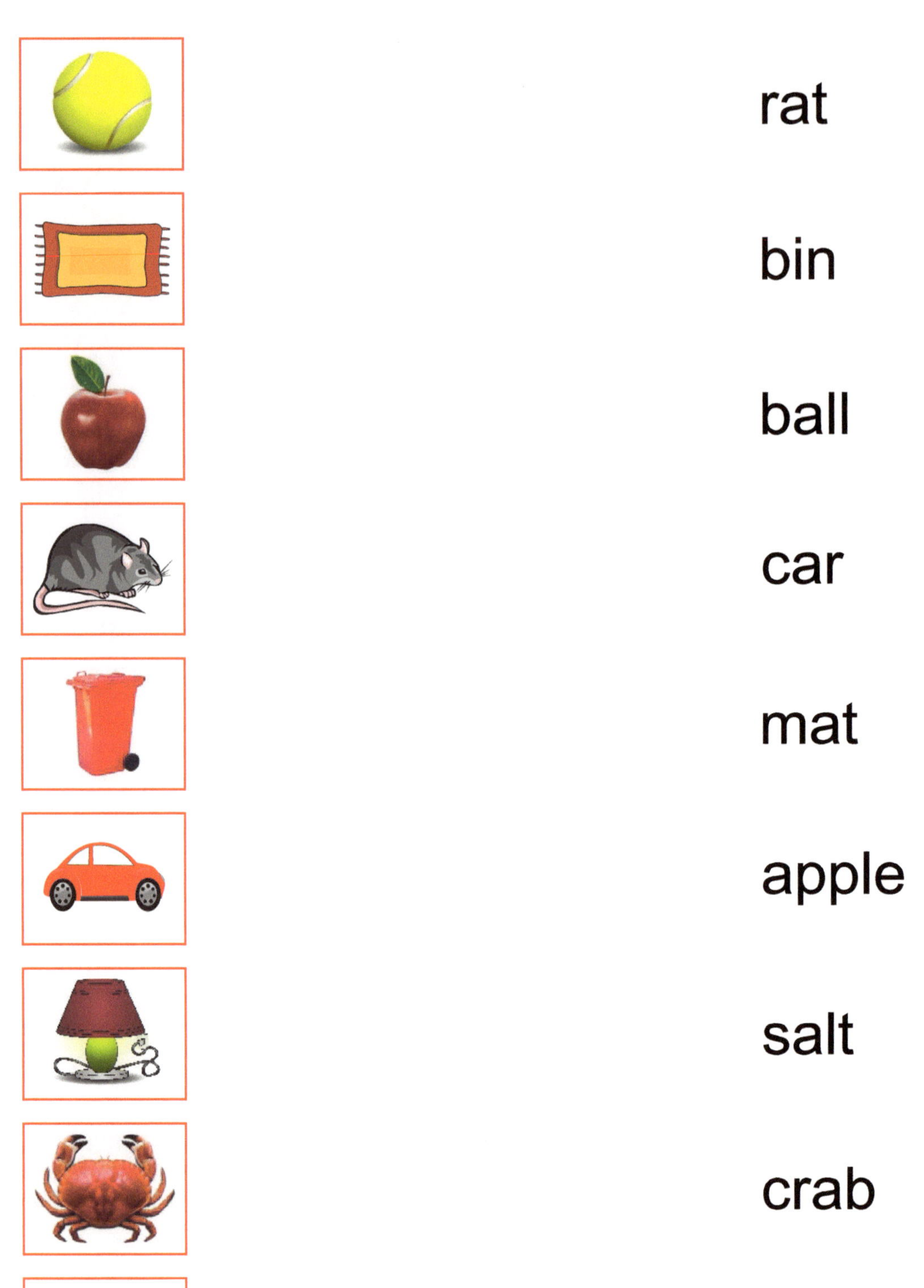

Read and Match

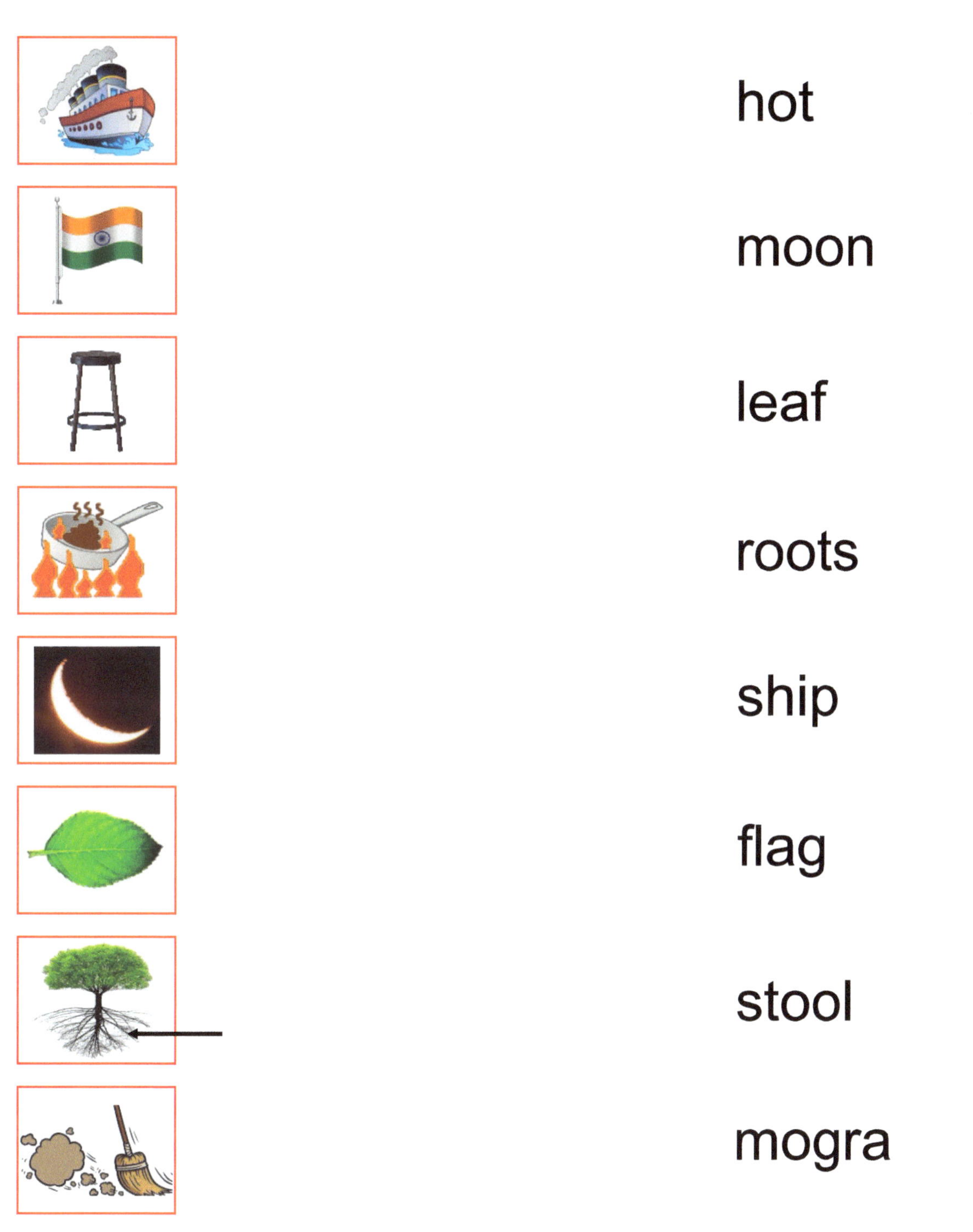

Read and Match

roof

six

ten

lid

nib

egg

dog

mint

bucket

Read and Match

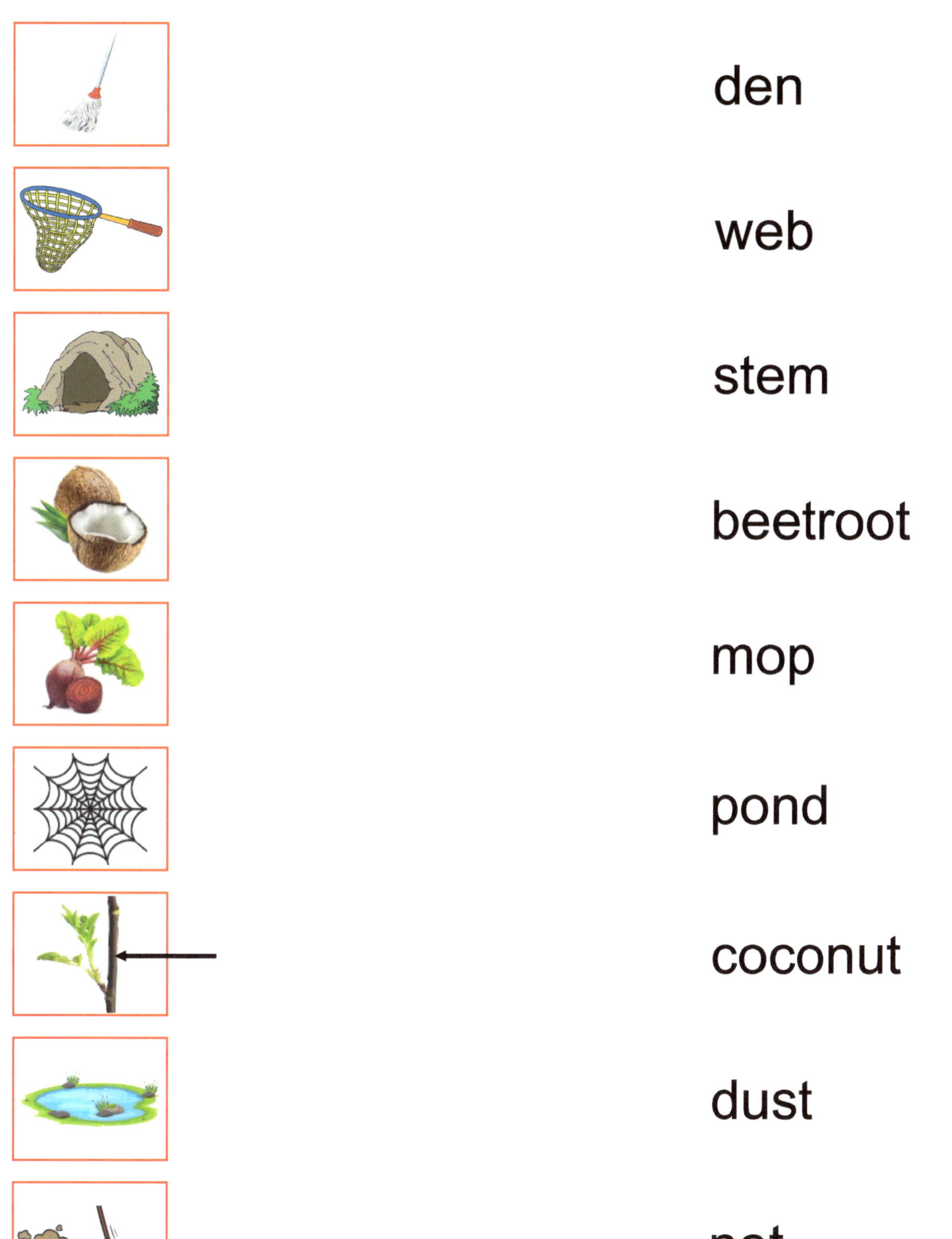

den

web

stem

beetroot

mop

pond

coconut

dust

net

Read and Match

stamp

drum

shed

sharp

bus

lost

belt

bulb

swan

Read and Match

Read and Match

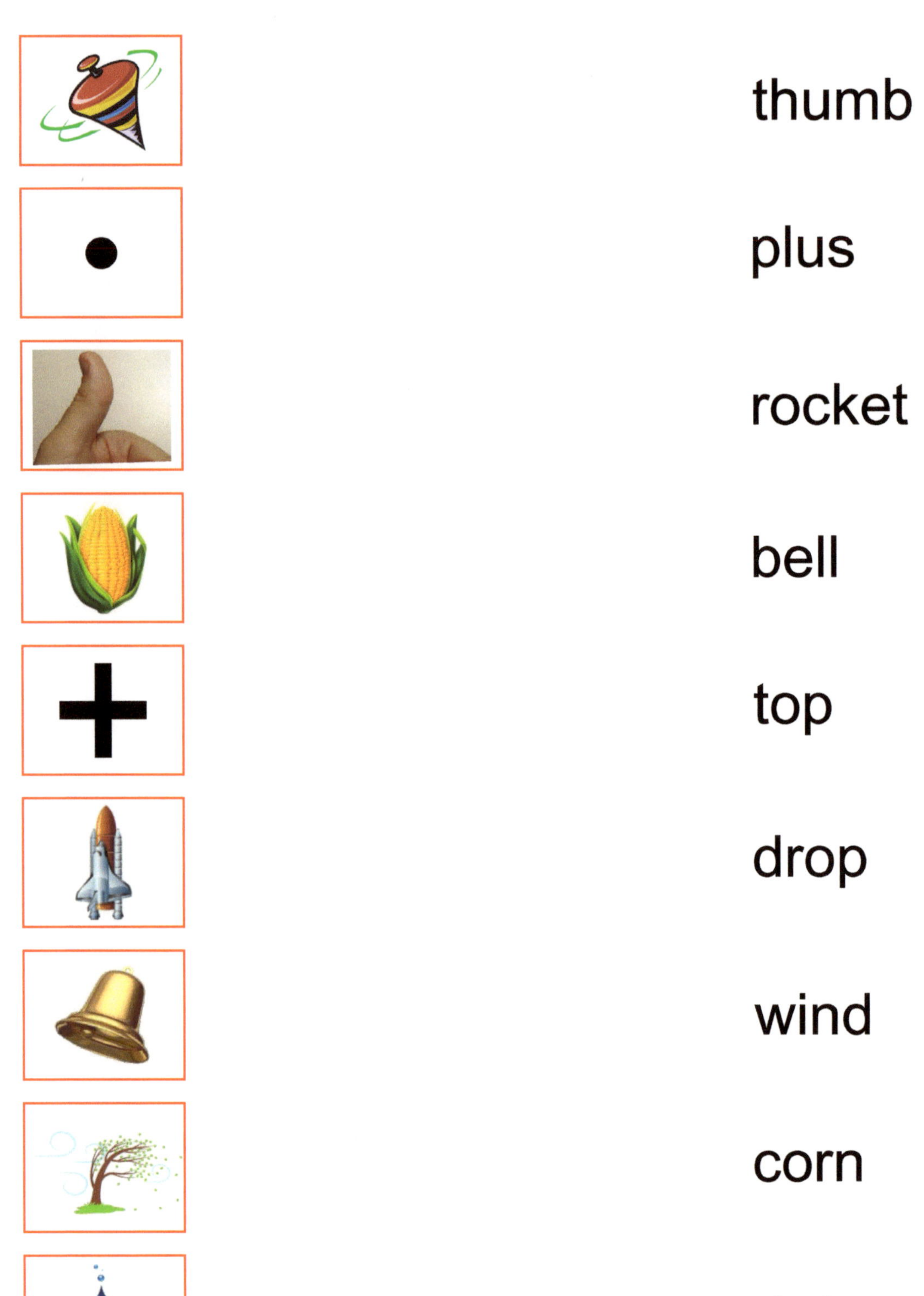

thumb

plus

rocket

bell

top

drop

wind

corn

dot

Read and Match

foot

frog

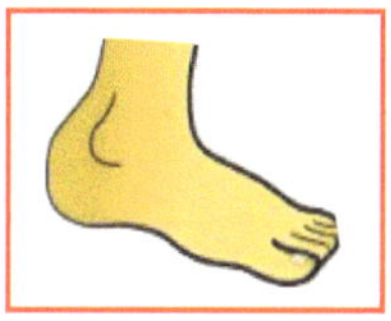

ball

zip

dent

clap

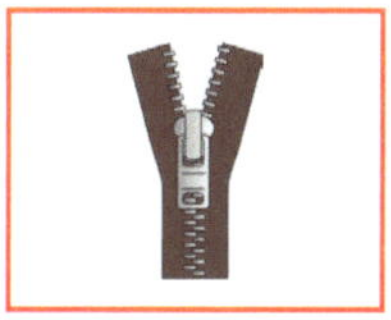

cold

jam

balloon

Read and Match

Read and Match

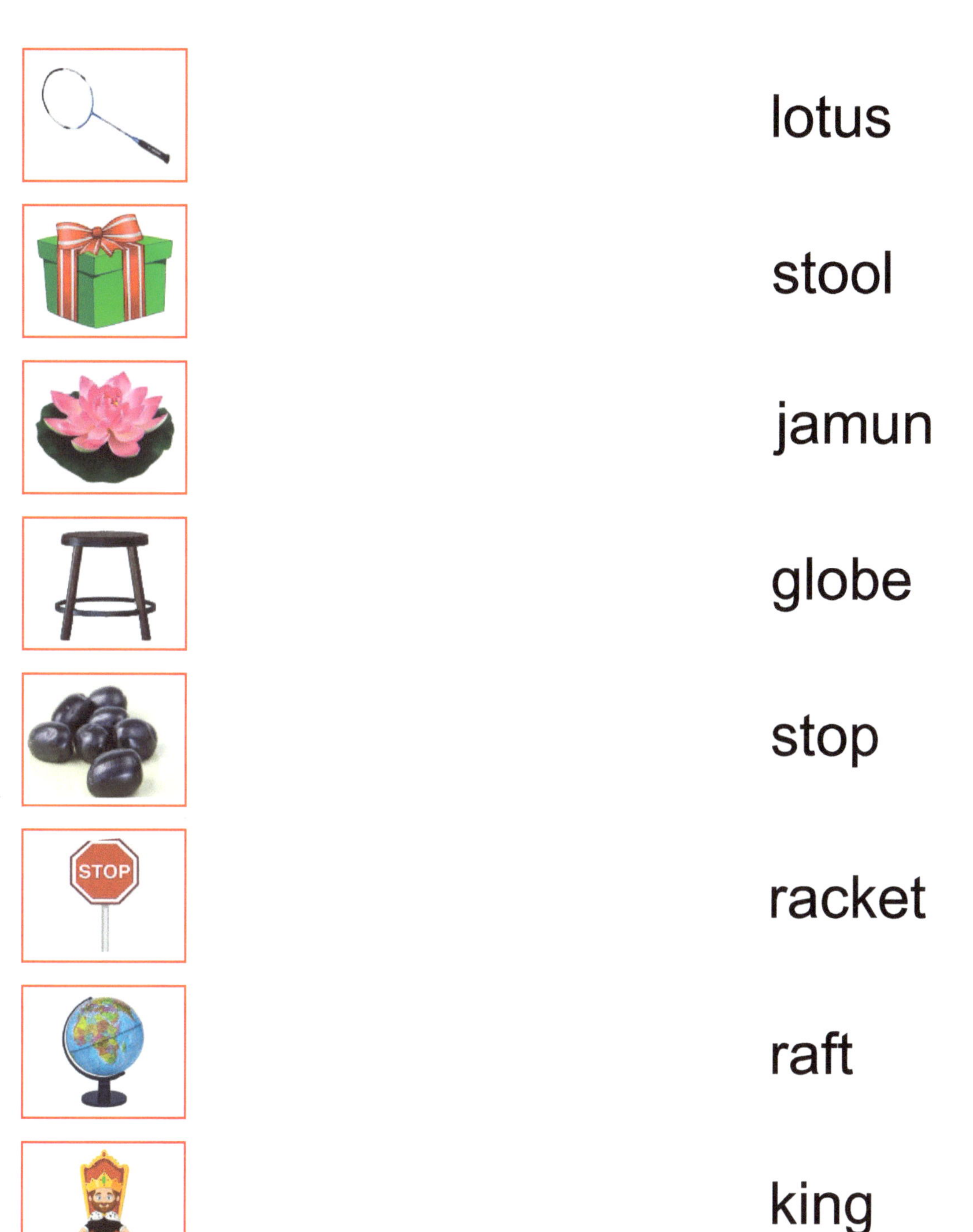

Read and Match

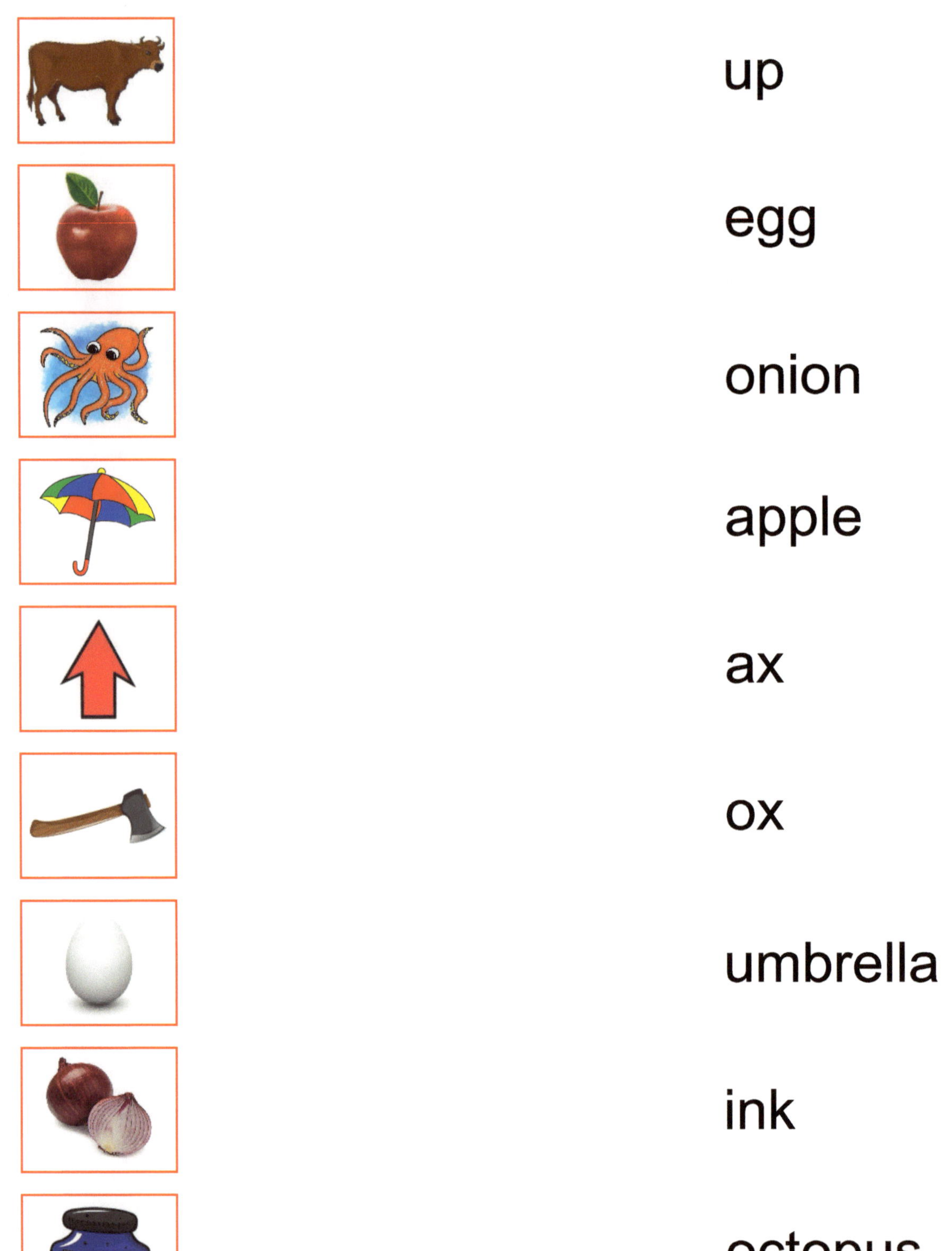

Read and Match

jug

boat

goggle

pot

fan

zigzag

tong

quill

desk

Read and Match

 watch

 rocket

 cup

 nine

 moon

 bank

 sun

 vegetable

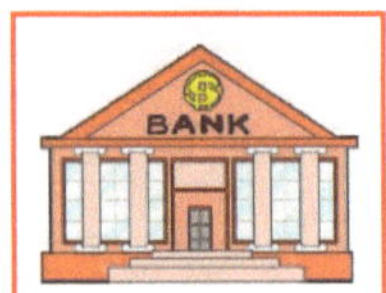 tree

Read and Match

golf

pink

pump

jump

last

mask

colt

rust

dump

Read and Match

Read and Match

Read and Match

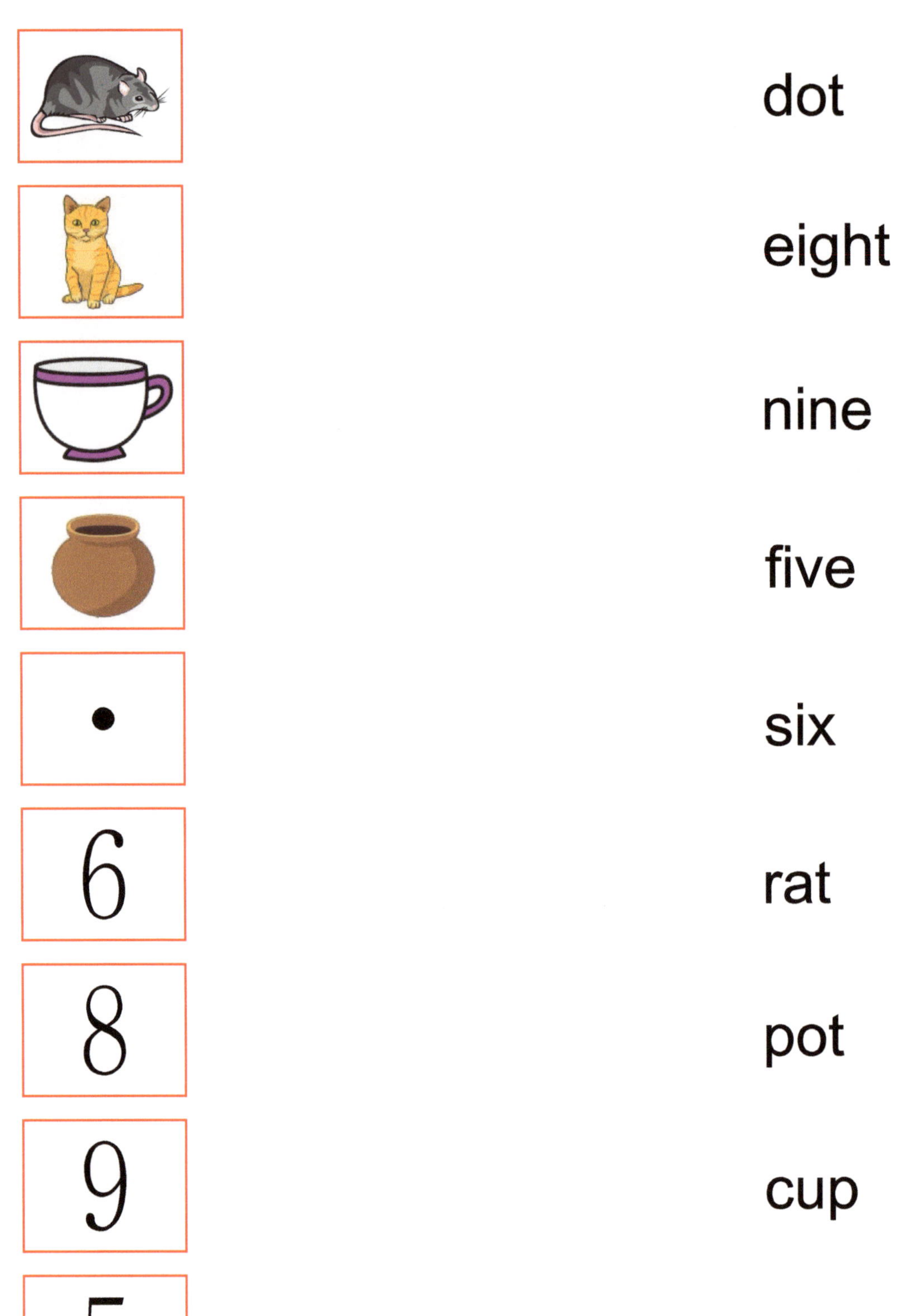

Read and Match

Read and Match

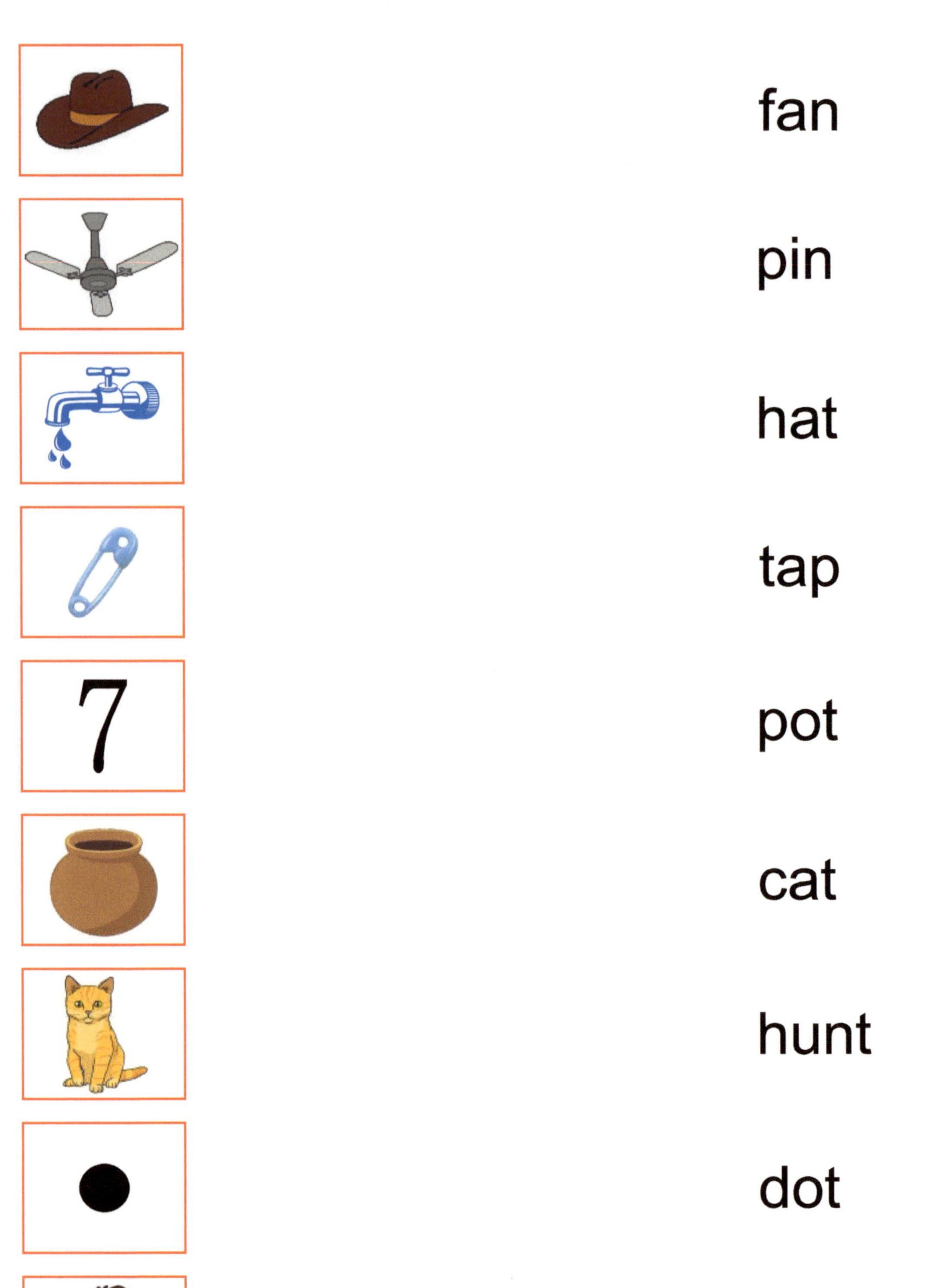

fan

pin

hat

tap

pot

cat

hunt

dot

seven

Read and Match

den

jug

pant

oil

nib

tag

hot

pen

gift

Read and Match

guava

banana

papaya

jamun

mango

watermelon

pineapple

kiwi

pomegranate

Read and Match

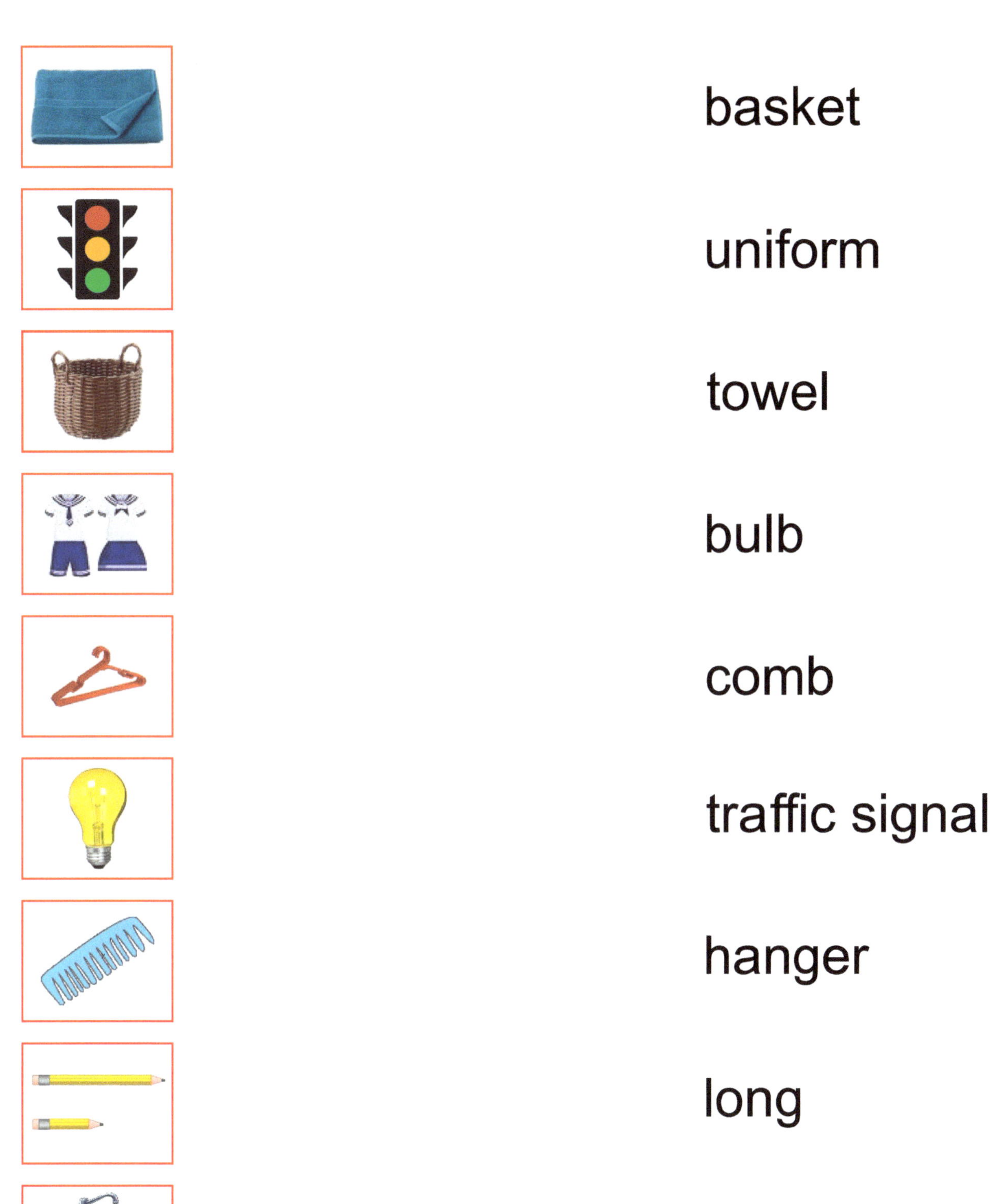

Read and Match

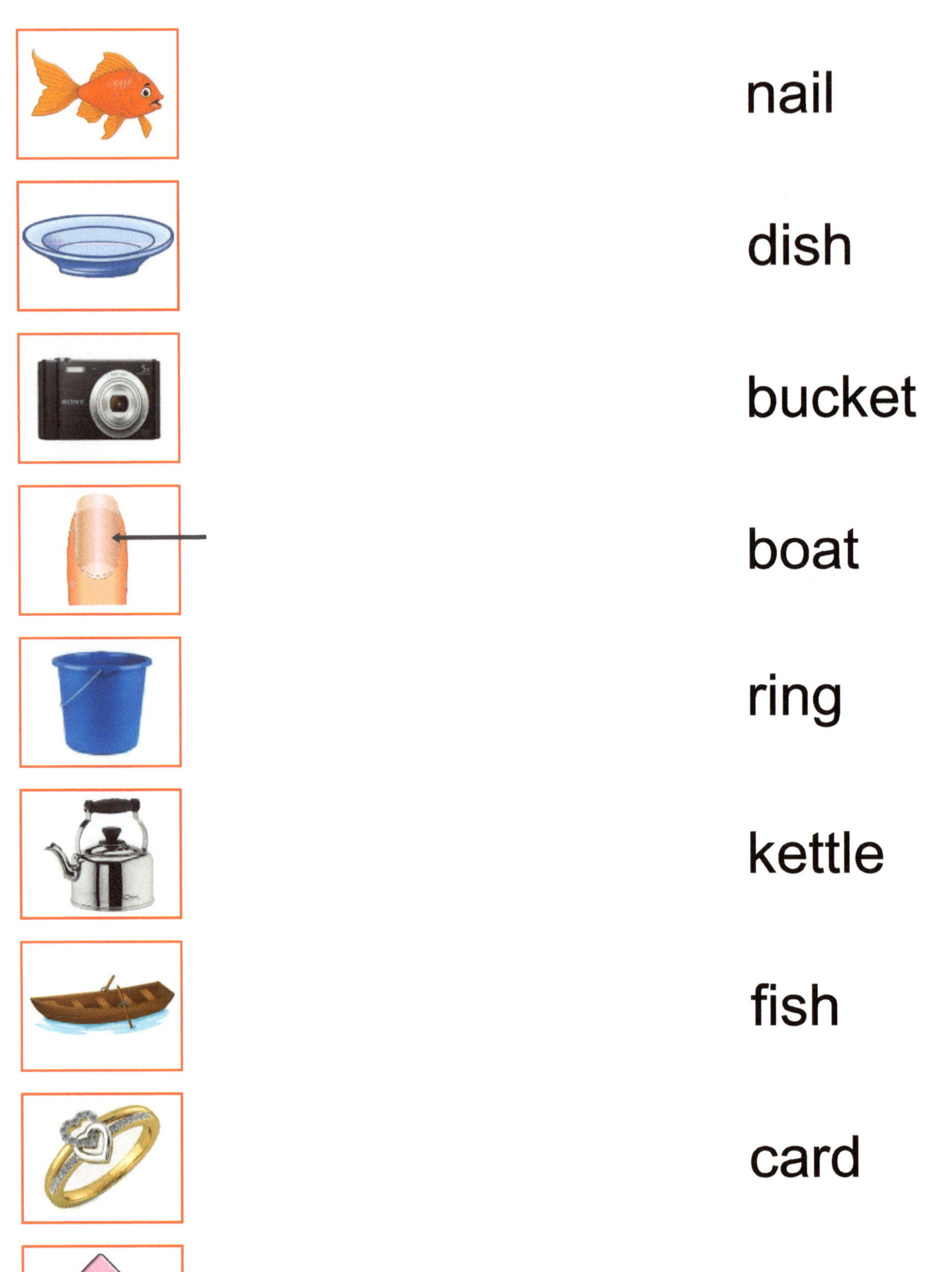

nail

dish

bucket

boat

ring

kettle

fish

card

camera

Read and Match

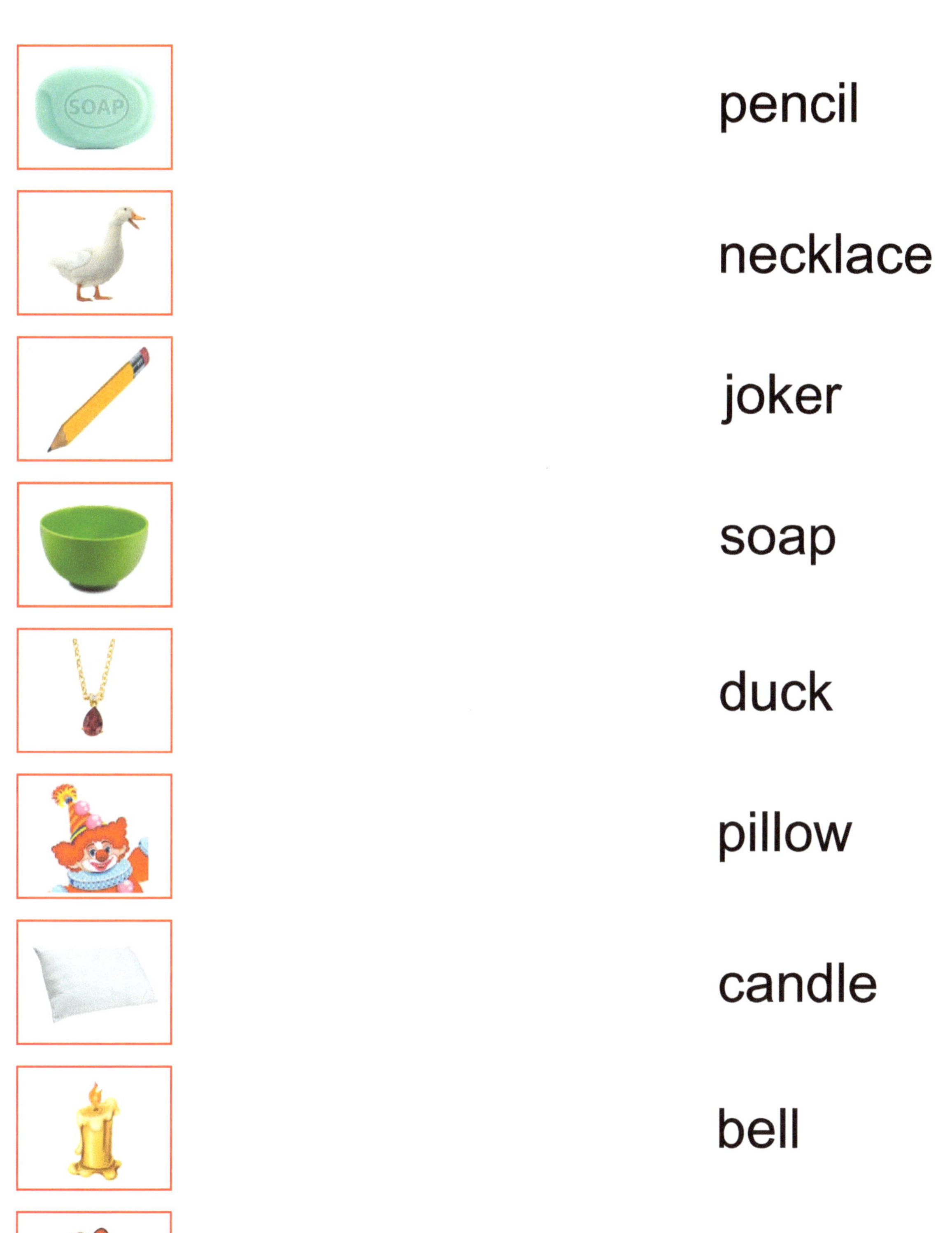

Read and Match

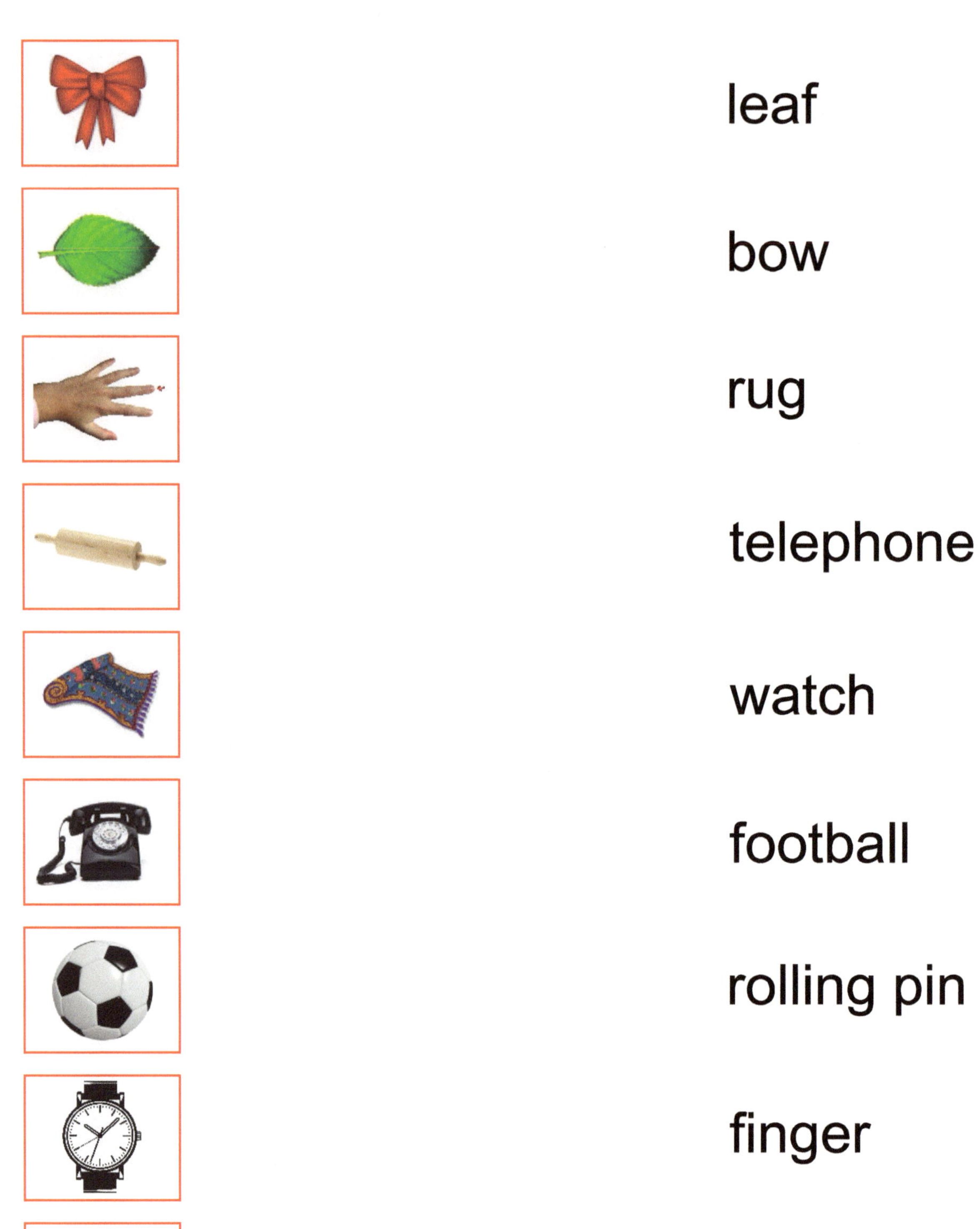

leaf

bow

rug

telephone

watch

football

rolling pin

finger

cold

Read and Match

socket

cake

well

zip

leg

racket

ring

dark

lock

Read and Match

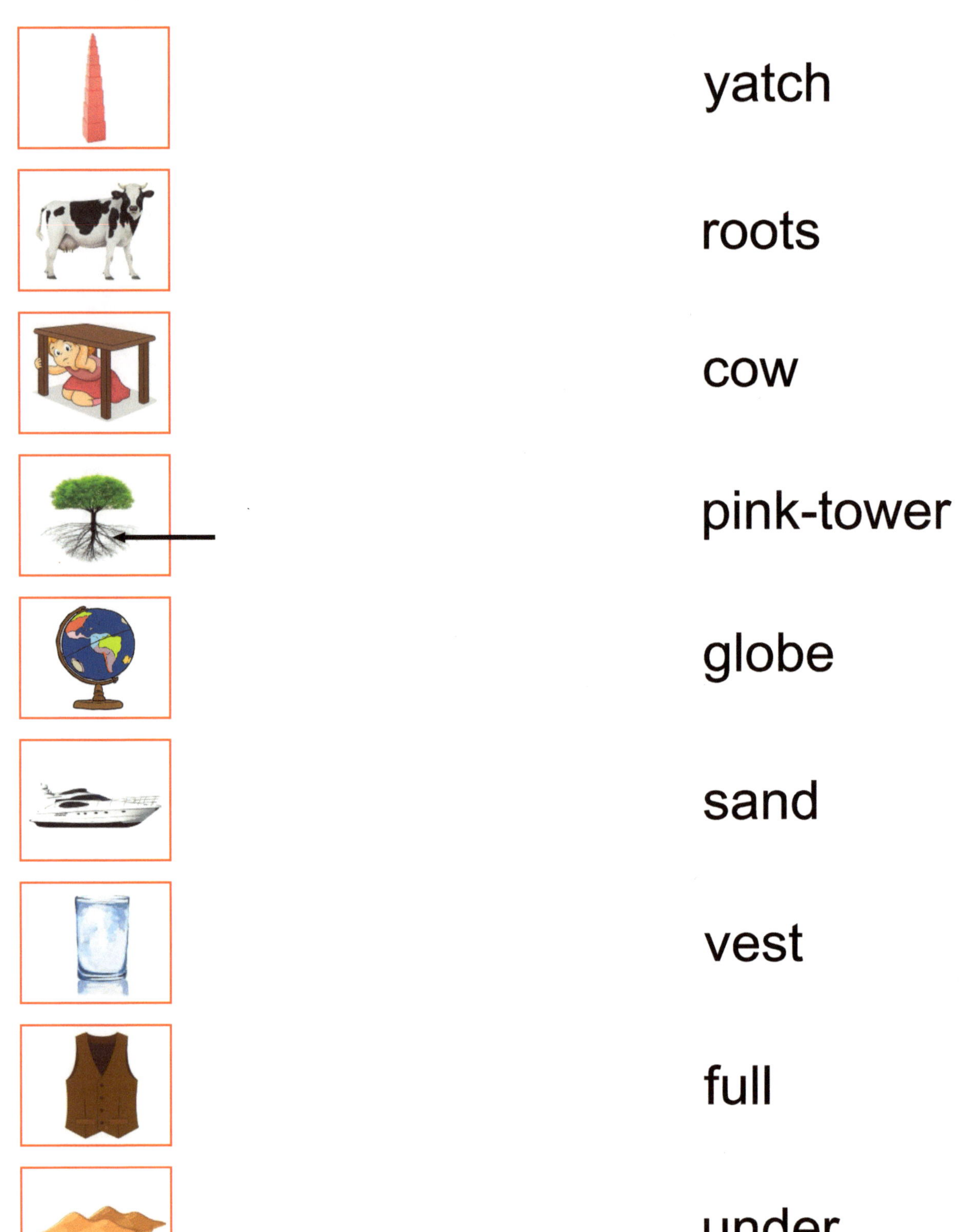

Read and Match

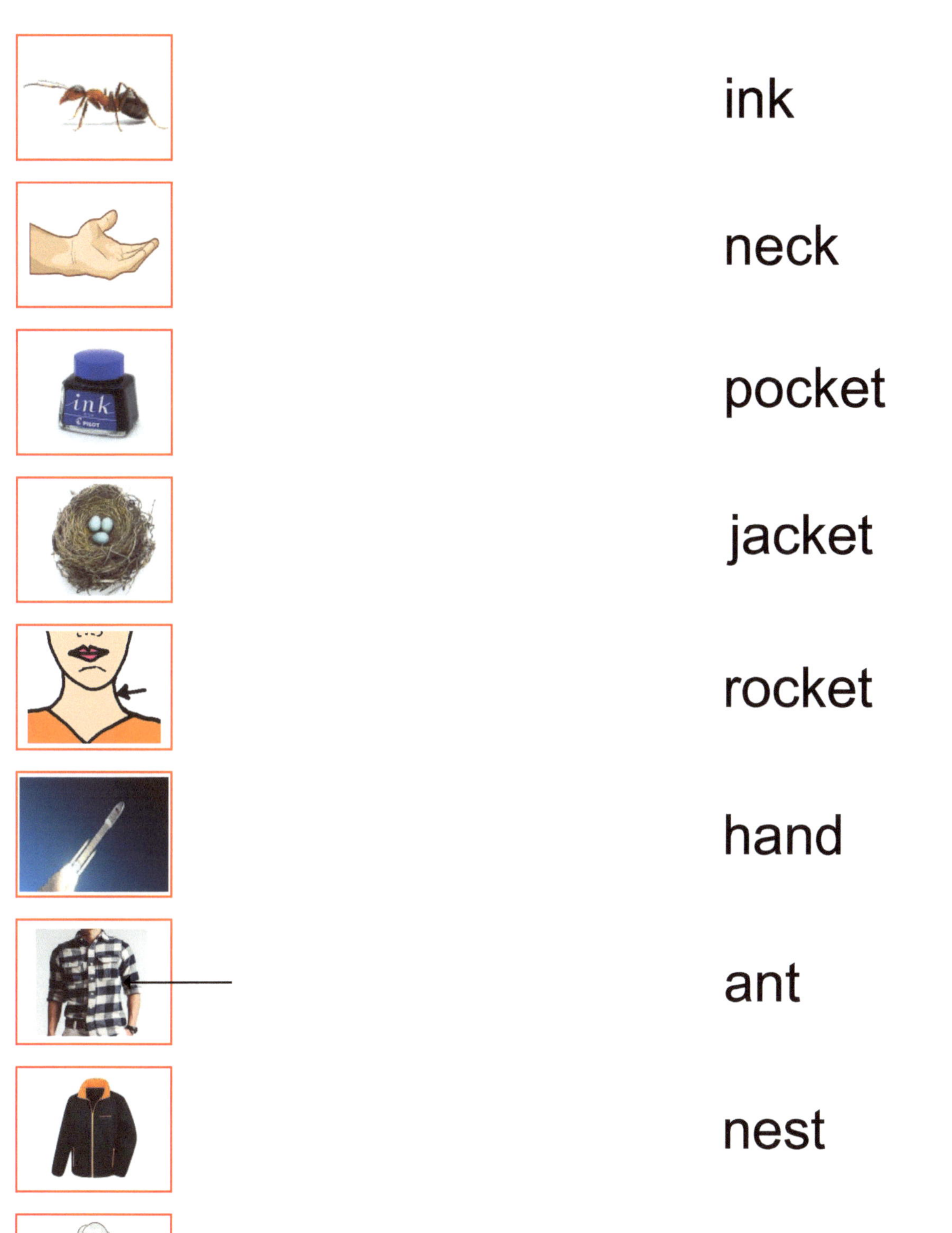

ink

neck

pocket

jacket

rocket

hand

ant

nest

fist

Read and Match

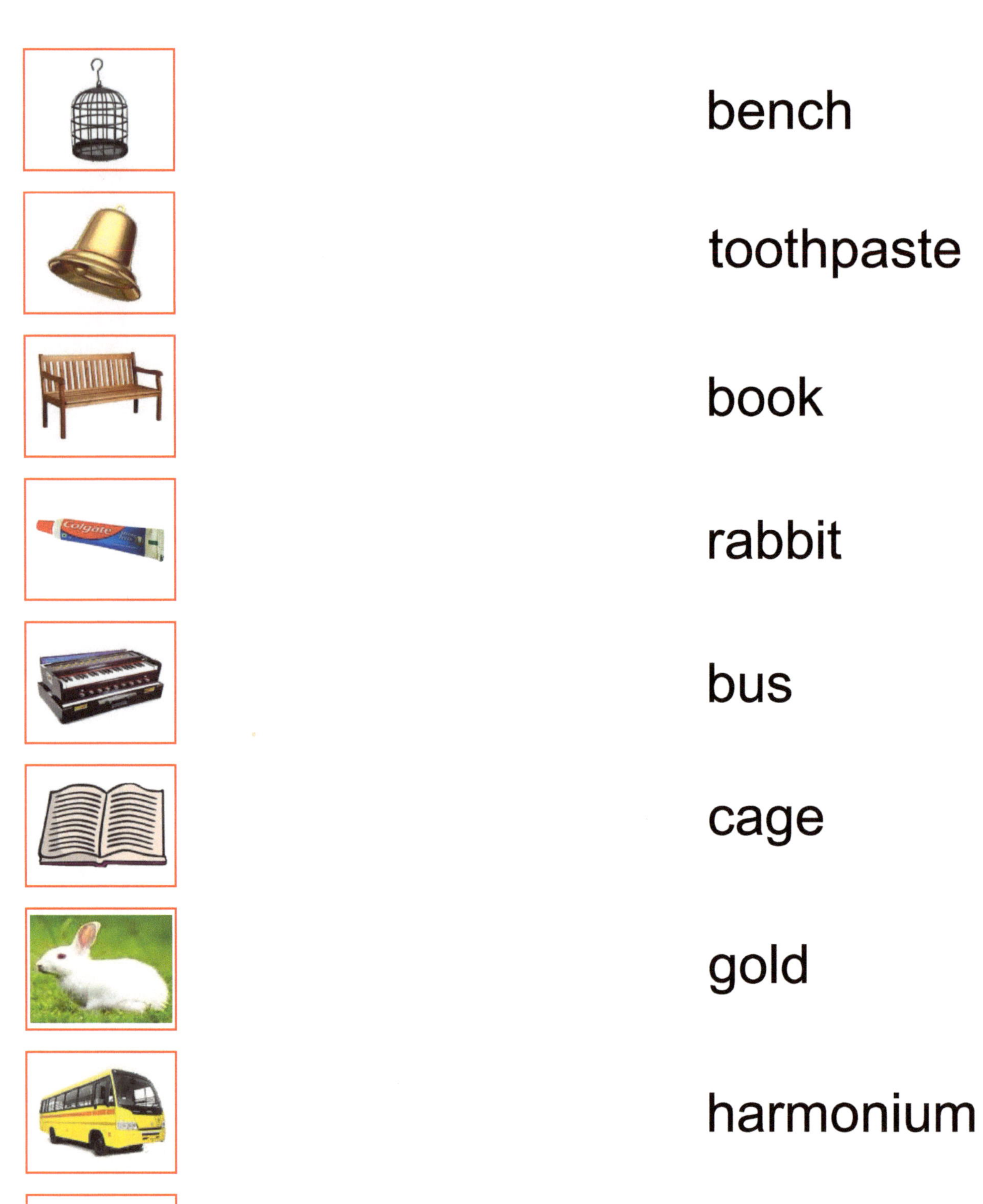

bench

toothpaste

book

rabbit

bus

cage

gold

harmonium

bell

Read and Match

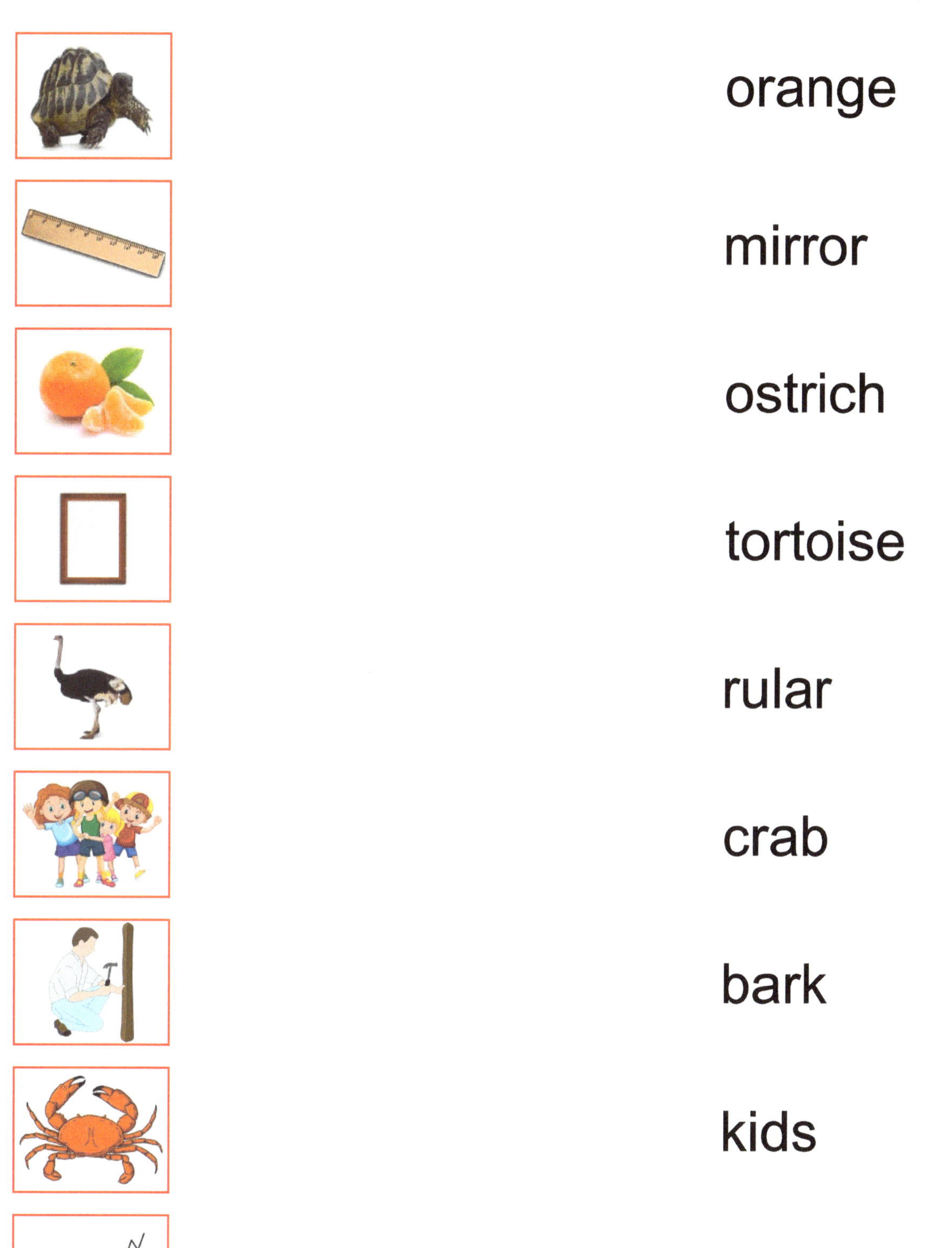

orange

mirror

ostrich

tortoise

rular

crab

bark

kids

fix

Read and Match

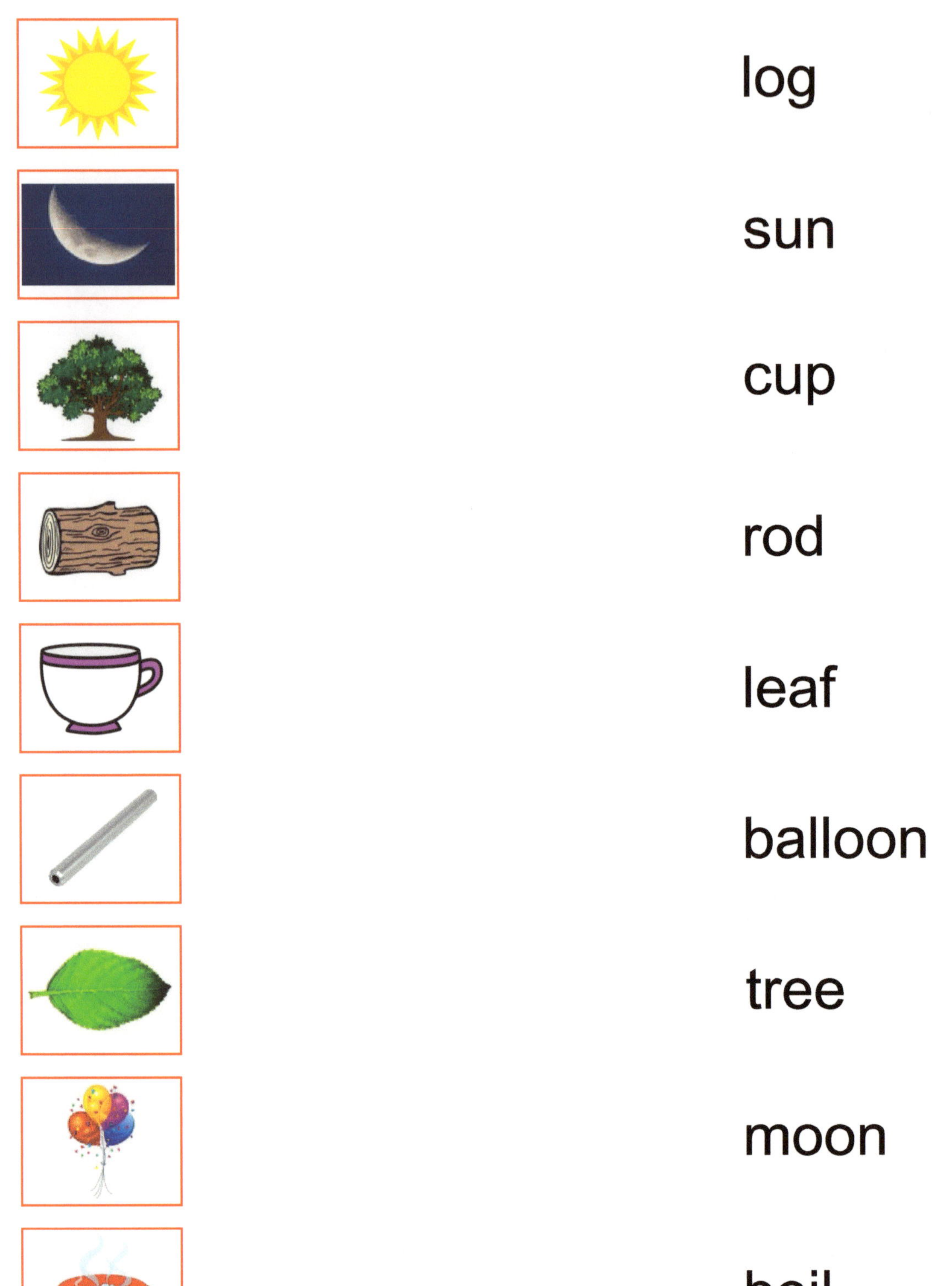

Read and Match

 lolipop

 igloo

 octopus

 nose

 cloude

 elephant

 arrow

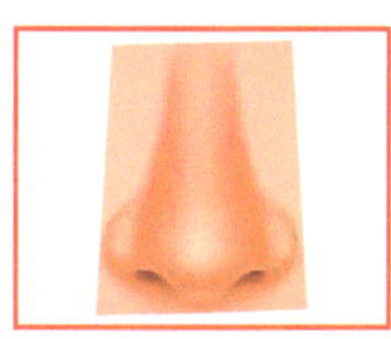 wall

 tree

Read and Match